Foreword

In the past, research programs funded by the Department of Defense (DoD) often led industry efforts in technology. Today the reverse is largely the case—technology leadership has shifted to industry, where most research and development (R&D) dollars are spent.

> "Budget pressures have squeezed military R&D spending in recent years... down 30% from its inflation-adjusted peak in 1989. Meanwhile, the private sector's share of total R&D expenditures in the U.S. is soaring. In 1960, private-sector R&D spending amounted to roughly one-third of the country's total. In 1999, it accounted for two thirds (an estimated $166 billion). Over the same period, the military's share dropped to 16% from 53%."[1]

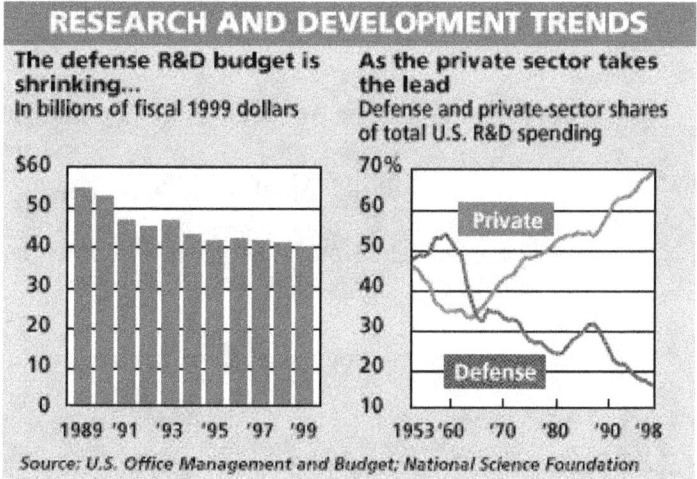

RESEARCH AND DEVELOPMENT TRENDS

The defense R&D budget is shrinking...
In billions of fiscal 1999 dollars

As the private sector takes the lead
Defense and private-sector shares of total U.S. R&D spending

Source: U.S. Office Management and Budget; National Science Foundation

Challenges to the Government today are to find ways to entice commercial industry into collaborating with the Department in vital research efforts, and to acquire commercial products using commercially friendly terms. While the acquisition streamlining legislation of the 1990s went a long way to create more commercial-like contracting processes for the Government, some practices from past decades are holdovers to today. One such area is intellectual property (IP).

The concept of IP is fundamental to a capitalist society. A company's interest in protecting its IP from uncompensated exploitation is as important as a farmer's interest in protecting his or her seed corn. Often companies will not consider jeopardizing their vested IP to comply with the Government contract clauses that have remained in use since the days when DoD was the technology leader and frequent funder of research programs. We must now create a new environment for

---

[1] Chen, Kathy (November 12, 1999). "Pentagon Finds Fewer Firms Want to Do Military R&D." *Wall Street Journal*, Sec. A, p. 20, Col. 1.

negotiating IP terms and conditions that protect the true interest of the Government—incorporating technologically advanced solutions into the weapons systems and management systems we deploy. This guide was created for the Government acquisition community (i.e., contracting personnel, legal counsel, and program managers) and its industry partners as a tool to equip them with new ideas and solutions to address the IP issues that divide us in the negotiation process.

On September 5, 2000, the Under Secretary of Defense for Acquisition, Technology and Logistics [USD(AT&L)] signed a policy letter announcing a shift in focus for negotiating IP contract terms with commercial firms that ordinarily do not do business with DoD. This letter, found in Appendix A, begins the process of shifting our thinking and putting into place the mandate to develop training materials that will assist the acquisition community in this endeavor.

Subsequently, USD(AT&L) signed a letter on January 5, 2001 (also included in Appendix A) that added to this initiative. In addition to directing that this guide be published, it highlighted the importance of engaging in certain practices currently permitted by regulation, including

- emphasizing the use of specifically negotiated license rights,[2]

- exercising flexibility when negotiating patent rights,

- using performance-based acquisition strategies that may obviate the need for data and/or rights, and

- acquiring only data and/or rights to data truly needed for a given acquisition.

Additionally, the letter initiated an IP working group, comprised of Department personnel and industry advisors, to evaluate certain patent clause waiver possibilities and the use and protection of industry's proprietary data, and to revise Defense Federal Acquisition Regulation Supplement (DFARS) Part 227, Patents, Data, and Copyrights. Finally, it called for an aggressive education campaign.

This guide is intended to provide a straightforward discussion of the information contracting officers need to negotiate IP arrangements. Such negotiations should strive to balance the needs of the Government and industry, resulting in a win-win solution. This guide is not inclusive of all IP issues and is not meant to be a complete treatise on all nuances of IP. Rather, it is designed to provide

- a description of the fundamental principles and concepts of negotiating IP rights (Chapter 1);

---

[2] DFARS 227.7103-5 (d), Specifically Negotiated License Rights, commonly referred to as "special licenses."

- a foundational framework of IP's key aspects and its treatment in Government contracting (Chapter 2);

- a description of the various planning activities, especially market research, that may reduce IP-related problems later in the acquisition process (Chapter 3); and

- a description of the major IP issues that keep some companies from responding to Government solicitations, as well as possible solutions to attract their involvement (Chapter 4).

In addition, this guide provides background and reference materials, included as appendices:

- Appendix A ("USD(AT&L) Policy Letters") presents the policy context against which this guide was created.

- Appendix B ("IP Basics—Supplemental Materials") provides a general understanding of the IP basics, including trade secrets, copyrights, trademarks, patents, technical data, and computer software.

- Appendix C ("Federal Acquisition Regulation Clause Summary") provides an easy reference and summary analysis of all IP clauses contained in the Federal Acquisition Regulation (FAR).

- Appendix D ("Defense Federal Acquisition Regulation Supplement Clause Summary") provides an easy reference and summary analysis of all IP clauses contained in the DFARS.

- Appendix E ("History") provides a chronological history of patent law and describes how technical data requirements came into the procurement process.

- Appendix F ("References") lists IP-related educational materials and references for further reading.

- Appendix G ("Intellectual Property Resources") identifies key agency points of contact available to provide advice and strategies as needed.

Throughout this guide, the FAR and DFARS clauses relating to IP are discussed. The specific terms in this guide are primarily focused on FAR-based contracts. However, the solutions cited here can be applied, with appropriate legal counsel, to negotiating alternative vehicles such as "other transactions," cooperative agreements, cooperative research and development agreements (CRADAs), and grants.

This guide's primary focus is on the issues associated with nontraditional Defense contractors in commercial industry. Traditional Defense contractors have similar issues, but, because of their familiarity and long-standing involvement, they have a better working understanding of the FAR and DFARS clauses. With either non-traditional or traditional contractors, the Government's policy is to obtain only the minimum necessary rights.

Contents

Chapter 1
The Principles

When acquiring intellectual property (IP) license rights, the Department of Defense (DoD) acquisition community should consider certain core principles. The table below highlights these principles and is followed by more details on each. For the purposes of this guide, the term "intellectual property" means patents, copyrights, trademarks, and trade secrets. In dealing with IP rights, the Government has promulgated policies and regulations on patents, copyrights, technical data, and computer software.

Core IP Principles for the DoD Acquisition Community
1. Integrate IP considerations fully into acquisition strategies for advanced technologies in order to protect core DoD interests.
2. Respect and protect privately developed IP because it is a valuable form of intangible property that is critical to the financial strength of a business.
3. Resolve issues prior to award by clearly identifying and distinguishing the IP *deliverables* from the *license rights* in those deliverables.
4. Negotiate specialized IP provisions whenever the customary deliverables or standard license rights do not adequately balance the interests of the contractor and the Government.
5. Seek flexible and creative solutions to IP issues, focusing on acquiring only those deliverables and license rights necessary to accomplish the acquisition strategy.

1	Integrate IP considerations fully into acquisition strategies for advanced technologies in order to protect core DoD interests.

IP considerations have a critical impact on the cost and affordability of technology, and they should not be treated as a separate or distinct issue that can be negotiated apart from contract performance requirements or price/cost factors. Therefore, when developing acquisition strategies, be sure to consider all types of DoD requirements, such as production, acceptance testing, installation, operation, maintenance, upgrade or modification, interoperability with other systems, and transfer of technologies to other programs/systems/platforms. In particular, address IP matters when making source selection determinations and evaluating total ownership cost.

2	Respect and protect privately developed IP because it is a valuable form of intangible property that is critical to the financial strength of a business.

Innovation requires substantial financial investment and effort over a long period of time and uses scarce resources. To make this investment worthwhile, industry relies on its IP rights as the primary means to recoup these nonrecurring costs and seek profit. A developer's IP rights ensure that the developer has the exclusive right to exploit his or her innovation commercially and financially, with the understanding that the technology must be embodied in products or services that will ensure a return on the investment. The end result of protecting IP rights is that technology is advanced and disseminated widely, and innovators are rewarded for their efforts.

The Government should honor the rights in IP resulting from private developments and limit its demands to IP rights for essential Government purposes. The Government also should encourage the maximum practical commercial use of inventions made while performing Government contracts, and it generally should encourage the use of U.S. patents in performing Government contracts and subcontracts. The Government often acquires supplies or services on a competitive basis; nevertheless, it must ensure the protection of privately developed IP in the process.

Subcontractors are vital members of the technology team and may deal directly with the Government on matters related to rights in IP. Prime contractors are required to flow down to their subcontractors the clauses needed for IP protection. Furthermore, prime contractors may not, as a condition for award, require subcontractors to relinquish their rights in their IP.

The unauthorized or inadvertent disclosure of a trade secret may destroy the (commercial) value of that trade secret. This is equally true for both solicited and unsolicited proposals. Many legal remedies for inappropriate disclosures of trade secrets exist, including money damages, injunctions, and criminal sanctions. However, standard contractual remedies for the inappropriate disclosure of a trade secret are often inadequate to preserve the value of the trade secret because it is difficult to prove their misappropriation. As a result, most commercial businesses simply refuse to allow another party access to their trade secrets unless that party has provided adequate assurances that the trade secrets will be handled and protected according to the best commercial standards. Therefore, DoD must utilize all available means for safeguarding restricted IP, including employee training for the handling of restricted materials, technological access or copying protection, and physical access restrictions.

> **3   Resolve issues prior to award by clearly identifying and distinguishing the IP *deliverables* from the *license rights* in those deliverables.**

IP terms and conditions are core elements of the deal when developing or acquiring cutting-edge technologies. They are integral aspects of performance requirements and cost or price, and they will have a lasting impact on life-cycle support for that technology. As with any critical issue, the parties must have a meeting of the minds prior to executing the contract. They are more likely to quickly find mutually agreeable terms and conditions during preaward phases.

The standard FAR and DFARS clauses require that certain information be set forth in the contract (e.g., the preaward listing of proprietary IP). If that information is incomplete or ambiguous, the clauses will not be effective. It is not enough merely to incorporate the standard FAR and DFARS clauses, because they do not always resolve critical IP issues. For example, there is no clause establishing rights in commercial computer software. However, the DFARS establishes procedures for the early identification of restrictions on noncommercial technical data and computer software. Similar processes should be established for commercial technologies and other important IP concerns.

"IP deliverables" refers to the contractual obligation to deliver IP that has a predetermined content and format. The Government may own the delivered physical medium on which the IP resides, but generally it will not own the IP rights. "License rights" refers to the Government's ability to use, reproduce, modify, and release the delivered IP. These two concepts are integrally related. Using creative flexibility in both areas will result in a win–win agreement.

It is important to take steps early in the acquisition process to identify commercial software and technical data that will be delivered. When acquiring commercial software and technical data, DoD normally receives only those deliverables and associated license rights that are customarily provided to the public. However, there is no standard clause for commercial computer software; the parties must incorporate the relevant license agreement into the contract, taking care to ensure that its provisions are understood and are in keeping with the Government's needs.

> **4   Negotiate specialized IP provisions whenever the customary deliverables or standard license rights do not adequately balance the interests of the contractor and the Government.**

A "one-size-fits-all" license agreement will likely include terms and conditions that are inapplicable or irrelevant to a particular acquisition or program. This creates inefficiencies and may force parties to take unnecessarily restrictive positions on other important contract terms (e.g., price) to account for the imbalance. When negotiating, distinguish "off-the-shelf" or non-developmental acquisitions from development partnerships.

Commercial software should be acquired using the commercial license terms whenever these terms are available. Changes in commercial license terms should be negotiated only when there is a specific Government need that must be addressed and when the Government is willing to pay the cost associated with that particular Government need. Negotiators should not assume that changes in commercial license agreements can be made at no cost.

5	**Seek flexible and creative solutions to IP issues, focusing on acquiring only those deliverables and license rights necessary to accomplish the acquisition strategy.**

DoD policy is to require delivery of only the technical data and computer software necessary to satisfy agency needs. The Government should avoid requiring delivery of technical data and computer software "just in case." Rather, to accommodate potential future needs for technical data and computer software, the Government might explore contingency-based delivery requirements, like a special contract provision that would define the types of technical data and computer software that the Government might wish to order in the future. Also, with regard to technical data and computer software deliverables, the delivery needs or requirements should be separated from the technical data and computer software that is needed only for viewing (e.g., other programmatic data in the contractor's facility). When acquiring software, rights in that software are the *primary* deliverable to the Government. For commercial technical data and computer software, the Government should seek only that data normally provided to a commercial customer—typically far less than that provided under traditional DoD contracts.

As a general rule under Government contracts, the contractor-developer is allowed to retain ownership of the technical data and computer software it developed; and the Government receives only a license to use that technical data and computer software. DoD does not "own" the technical data and computer software included in deliverables, even if the Department paid for 100 percent of the development costs. The scope of the license depends on the nature of the technical data and computer software, the relative source of funding for development, and the negotiations between the parties.

Finally, program officials should seek to establish performance-based requirements that enhance long-term competitive interests, in lieu of acquiring detailed design data and data rights.

SUMMARY

These guiding principles require fair treatment of IP owners and encourage the use of that IP to produce commercial products and services that meet Defense needs. They support the current movement for DoD to collaborate with industry on more commercially friendly terms, so that the benefits of commercial research and development can be more readily assimilated into Defense products.

Chapter 2
Intellectual Property Framework

INTELLECTUAL PROPERTY

The American Heritage® Dictionary of the English Language, Fourth Edition (2000), defines "intellectual property" as "A product of the intellect that has commercial value...." IP is thus the physical manifestation of original thought. Its value, expressed through technology and industrial innovation, is central to the economic, environmental, and social well-being of the United States and offers many benefits. Some such benefits include

- improved standard of living,

- increased public- and private-sector productivity,

- the creation of new industries and employment opportunities,

- improved public services, and

- enhanced competitiveness of U.S. products in world markets.

It is important to understand that IP is a form of *intangible* personal property, which must be carefully distinguished from the tangible/physical items or products that include or "embody" that IP. For example, when a person buys a book at the local bookstore, that person acquires ownership of that single, physical copy of the book but does not acquire ownership of the intangible IP rights (in this case, most likely copyright) that may protect the contents of the book.

Due to the intangible nature of IP, the value of any IP is limited to what the courts and legislatures are willing to protect against unauthorized use. In the United States, the parameters of what is—or is not—protected as IP are defined through an extensive collection of statutes, court opinions, legal rules, regulations, and procedures. Generally speaking, IP law is divided into categories according to the form of the human intellect product and the exclusive rights and remedies afforded the producers of that product. These categories are patents, copyrights, trade secrets, trademarks, and service marks.[1] In addition, two other less common forms of IP protection exist under Title 17 of the U.S. Code. They are mask works, which protect the patterns used in fabricating integrated circuits on semiconductor chips; and vessel hull designs, which protect the artistic or distinctive

---

[1] These categories—patents, copyrights, trade secrets, trademarks, and service marks—are summarized in Table 2.1, which can be found at the end of Chapter 2 (also see Appendix B for additional details).

aspects of certain vessel hulls, plugs, or molds. Consult your IP counsel regarding these forms of IP, as they are complex and specific to certain procurements and are not examined in this guide.

THE GOVERNMENT'S TREATMENT OF INTELLECTUAL PROPERTY

Statutory Citation and Regulatory Coverage

The statutory provisions for U.S. patent law are found exclusively in Title 35 of the U.S. Code. Copyright law is in Title 17 of the U.S. Code.

FAR Part 27 prescribes policies, procedures, and contract clauses pertaining to patents and directs agencies to develop coverage for rights in data and software. DFARS Part 227 provides the related policy guidance for Defense contracts. In general, under the FAR and DFARS, the Government acquires certain rights (subject to negotiation) in IP that is created in the performance of work under a Government contract or subcontract.

Current Department of Defense Framework

DoD clauses related to IP are currently built around the following framework:

◆ Contractors are generally permitted to retain ownership (e.g., title) of the IP rights governing the technologies/information that they develop or deliver under DoD contracts; and

◆ DoD receives only a (nonexclusive) license to use that IP—the scope of the license depends on the nature of the data, the relative source of funding for development, and negotiation between the parties.

The DoD approach categorizes IP into two main categories, most commonly referred to as "patent rights" and "technical data and computer software rights."

PATENT RIGHTS—RIGHTS IN INVENTIONS AND PATENTS

Patent rights refer to the Government's rights to "practice" an invention that is, or will be, protected by a US patent. It is important to distinguish between "subject inventions" and "background inventions."

A "subject invention" is an invention that is first "made"[2] during the performance of a Government contract. The Government's and contractor's rights and obligations concerning subject inventions are set forth in great detail in the standard

---

[2] An invention is "made" if it is either conceived or first actually reduced to practice under the contract. See 35 U.S. Code 201, FAR 52.227-11(a), and -12(a). These criteria are discussed further in Chapter 4.

FAR patent rights clauses, which are based in part on statutory requirements. As discussed above, the general approach is that the contractor is permitted to retain title to the invention, and the Government receives a nonexclusive license to use that invention for Government purposes. It is critical to understand that the granting of a license to the Government for a patent first made during perform-ance of a Government contract is *not negotiable* in a FAR contract, grant, or co-operative agreement. However, the terms of that license may be negotiable, and therefore some potential solutions are raised in Chapter 4 to address industry's concerns.

A "background invention" is any invention—other than a subject invention—that is owned or licensed by the contractor, and that will be incorporated into contract deliverables. The contracting parties generally must take affirmative steps, as dis-cussed in Chapter 4, to fully address background invention issues. Such steps in-clude identifying relevant background inventions and related issues early—prior to award, if possible[3]; and working with IP counsel to establish the rights and re-strictions on the Government's use of those inventions.

These issues are addressed in FAR Part 27, which also includes detailed regula-tions protecting and indemnifying the Government in the event of patent in-fringement by a contractor. Part 27 also includes numerous regulations discussing the mechanics of paying royalties, identifying Government rights, and conducting follow-up activities by both the Government and the contractor.

TECHNICAL DATA AND COMPUTER SOFTWARE RIGHTS

DFARS Subparts 227.71 and 227.72 establish a DoD-unique process for acquir-ing IP license rights governing technical data or computer software that is devel-oped or delivered under a contract. The license restricts the Government's use of the information contained in the deliverable.

In general, the contractor-developer retains title to the IP, and the Government receives a nonexclusive license to use, reproduce, modify, release, perform, dis-play, or disclose the data or software. The specific license granted depends on whether the technical data or computer software qualifies as noncommercial or commercial technology:

- ◆ Noncommercial Technology. The DFARS approach defines a set of stan-dard license categories that vary according to the parties' relative financial investments in the development of the underlying technology. If these standard rights do not effectively balance the parties' interests, specifically negotiated licenses are encouraged.[4]

---

[3] See Chapter 2 section titled "Early Identification of IP Restrictions and Related Issues."

[4] The key aspects of this approach are set forth in Table 2.2, which can be found at the end of Chapter 2.

- Commercial Technology. When acquiring commercial technologies, DoD normally receives only those deliverables and associated license rights that are customarily provided to the public. In fact, there is no DFARS clause prescribed for commercial computer software; the parties must incorporate the negotiated license agreement, including any specialized requirements, into the contract.[5]

EARLY IDENTIFICATION OF INTELLECTUAL PROPERTY RESTRICTIONS AND RELATED ISSUES

Many DoD acquisitions will involve a mix of commercial and noncommercial technologies. In these situations, it is important to ensure the contract includes provisions to cover both types of technologies and to include a statement clarifying how they apply to the deliverables (e.g., the noncommercial and commercial items can be segregated into separate line items, with each line item being governed by the appropriate clauses or attached license agreements).

This approach is unique to DoD and involves multiple forms of IP and a variety of license categories. The following areas, each of which is discussed below, are of particular interest in regards to understanding how to address DoD's approach to IP.

- Early identification of IP restrictions and related issues,

- Distinguishing IP deliverables from license rights,

- Specifically negotiated license agreements, and

- Markings and restrictive legends.

One of the simplest and yet most important aspects of acquiring IP is identifying the critical issues prior to contract award. Taking steps to identify and resolve these key issues early will benefit all parties, by

- Ensuring the contractor's ability to preserve valuable IP interests by asserting restrictions on trade secret information;

- Facilitating source selection by identifying IP-based restrictions that may impact the overall life-cycle cost of competing technologies;

- Facilitating structured negotiations by ensuring that the parties are fully aware of the critical IP issues; and

---

[5] The key aspects of this approach are set forth in Table 2.3, which can be found at the end of Chapter 2.

◆ Providing convenient methods for incorporating the results of IP negotiations into the contract.

However, the widespread belief that IP issues can be complex or contentious often results in delaying resolution of these matters until just before, or even after, contract award. The unfortunate result of this practice is that there may not be a "meeting of the minds" on core elements of the contract. Renegotiating such critical issues after award, when other related terms and conditions (e.g., cost or price factors, and performance tradeoffs) have already been "set," can be extremely difficult.

To avoid these problems, the DFARS prescribes certain mandatory pre- and post-award identification procedures, which should be supplemented whenever necessary to ensure that all key IP issues have been identified and resolved.

Defense Federal Acquisition Regulation Supplement Mandatory Listing Requirements

The DFARS includes a mandatory requirement for each offeror and contractor to identify, in a list, all noncommercial technical data and computer software that it plans to deliver with less-than-unlimited rights, and to assert specific restrictions on those deliverables. The listing requirement has both preaward and postaward phases, which are closely related:

◆ Preaward List. DFARS 252.227-7017 (the 7017 clause) requires prospective offerors to include the list, signed by a person with authority (to contractually bind the offeror) as part of the proposal. The Government may use the list during source selection to evaluate the impact of the identified restrictions on evaluation factors. If necessary, the Government may request additional information to evaluate the contractor's assertions. Upon contract award, it is critical that this list be attached to the contract.

◆ Postaward List. After contract award, any updates or changes to the preaward list are governed by paragraph (e) of the clauses DFARS 252.227-7013 and -7014. The contractor's ability to modify its assertions is limited to cases where a new assertion is based on new information or was inadvertently omitted from the preaward list but would not have materially affected source selection. No data/software may be delivered with restrictive markings unless identified on the list(s).

It is very important to check both preaward and postaward lists for accuracy and conformity. Paragraph (c) of the 7017 clause, and paragraph (e) of the 7013 and 7014 clauses, provide detailed guidance regarding the form and content of the lists (it is important to pay special attention to the asterisked notes). It also is important to note that the asserted restrictions are not immediately binding on the Government. The Government has up to three years after the completion or termination of the contract to respond to the assertions. However, assertions have some binding effect on the contractor, because the ability to raise new assertions is limited after award.

Supplemental Intellectual Property Listings

The mandatory DFARS listing requirement covers only asserted restrictions on deliverable *noncommercial* technical data and computer software. Depending on the nature of the acquisition plan for the technology (see Chapter 3), it may also be desirable to seek information pertaining to other forms of IP:

- ◆ Commercial Computer Software and Commercial Technical Data. In light of the general preference for acquiring commercial items, it is important to take steps to identify these commercial deliverables so that the Government can plan for maintenance and support. It may be extremely difficult to determine whether the absence of a particular data/software deliverable on the mandatory DFARS list is because it is being offered with unlimited rights, or because it is commercial data/software. If it is the latter, the associated reduction in IP deliverables and license rights may significantly impact the acquisition plan. To help identify and resolve these issues early, consider requiring a list of commercial data/software restrictions.

- ◆ Background Inventions. Even if all of the technical data and computer software is delivered with unlimited rights or Government-purpose rights (GPR), these deliverables may include background inventions, which may subject DoD to potential infringement liability for future uses that are contemplated by the acquisition plan. The license rights granted under the DFARS clauses covering rights in technical data and computer software do *not* grant rights in any inventions that may be incorporated into that data/software. These issues can be identified in a list of background inventions, which should identify (1) the U.S. patent or patent application covering the invention, (2) the contract deliverables that incorporate the invention, and (3) information regarding the license rights that the contractor is willing to grant to the Government for the background invention.

- ◆ Other Forms of Proprietary Information. There are other forms of valuable IP that may not be covered by any of the previously mentioned lists, such as a trade secret or copyrighted information that does not meet the definition of "technical data" or "computer software." These deliverables may qualify as "special works" or "existing works," or they may be some other form of company-proprietary information, such as financial, cost, business, or marketing information. When acquiring these deliverables, the contracting officer should consider requiring the contractor to identify and assert any restrictions on the Government's use thereof, similar to the 7017 list.

If these procedures are followed, the parties should be able to identify and resolve all critical IP issues before any significant problems develop. Generally speaking, most issues will center around either the IP deliverable requirements or the license rights associated with those deliverables.

DISTINGUISHING INTELLECTUAL PROPERTY *DELIVERABLES* FROM *LICENSE RIGHTS*

"IP deliverables" refers to the contractual obligation to deliver IP having a predetermined content and format. The Government may own the delivered physical medium on which the IP resides, but it generally will not own the IP rights. "License rights" refers to the Government's ability to use, reproduce, modify, and release the delivered IP. These two concepts are integrally related. Using creative flexibility in both areas will result in a win–win agreement.

Establishing Intellectual Property Deliverables—Content, Format, and Delivery Medium

DoD must ensure that the contract requires the delivery of all information that is necessary to accomplish each element of the acquisition strategy. It is important to realize that the standard DFARS clauses that establish the rights in technical data or computer software do not specify requirements. Therefore, when drafting delivery requirements for either technical data or computer software, it is important to specify

- ◆ Content (e.g., level of detail or nature of information),

- ◆ Recording/storage format (e.g., image files versus word processing format), and

- ◆ Delivery/storage medium (e.g., paper, CD-ROM, or on-line access).

In addition, when specifying delivery of technical data, the Government should carefully consider whether it needs the data to be delivered in a format necessary for use with a computer-aided design and/or computer-aided manufacturing system. Also, for computer software, it is critical to distinguish the human-readable source code from machine-readable object/executable code.

Options for Resolving Intellectual Property Deliverable Issues

There are a number of options available to structure mutually acceptable IP deliverable requirements:

- ◆ Altering the form or content of the deliverable. For example, the level of detail required might be reduced (e.g., requiring "form, fit, and function" data for detailed design data); or delivery might be required in a different format (e.g., drawings as CAD-CAM files as opposed to image files).

- ◆ Establishing life-cycle maintenance/support agreements with the original contractor-developer/supplier. This reduces or eliminates DoD's need for detailed design data for these purposes. Competition may be achieved by incorporating life-cycle support coverage into earlier procurement contracts.

- ◆ Providing for inspection of the data/software at the contractor's facility (e.g., see FAR 52.227-14 with its Alternate V; this civilian agency clause is not directly applicable to DoD but may serve as a model).

- ◆ Utilizing deferred ordering under DFARS 252.227-7027. This option permits DoD to require delivery of any data/software that was generated under the contract. The right expires 3 years after (1) acceptance of all items, or (2) termination of the contract. Also, see Chapter 4, Issue 7-A for issues and solutions regarding deferred ordering.

- ◆ Utilizing deferred delivery procedures under DFARS 252.227-7026. This provision may apply to any data/software that is designated in the contract. The right expires 2 years after (1) acceptance of all items, or (2) contract termination.

- ◆ Utilizing third-party escrow arrangements. These arrangements are used more commonly in the commercial arena, especially concerning computer software. Generally, the contractor-developer delivers a copy of the relevant "deliverable" to a neutral third party for safekeeping during a predefined escrow period. Within the escrow period, the Government may obtain delivery of the item if certain conditions occur. The parties must negotiate a number of important elements, such as the escrow period, the conditions under which the Government can require delivery, the procedures for requesting delivery, and the payment of escrow fees.

Although many IP issues may be resolved by tailoring the IP deliverable requirements, some matters will also require the negotiation of special license agreements.

SPECIFICALLY NEGOTIATED LICENSE AGREEMENTS

Remember: What may initially appear to be a license-rights issue may actually be solved by (1) modifying the IP deliverable requirements, (2) following the DFARS guidance concerning source of funding determinations at the lowest practicable level, and/or (3) verifying whether the data/software should be treated under commercial or non-commercial rules.

The parties should negotiate specifically negotiated license agreements (often called "special license agreements") whenever the customary deliverables or standard license rights do not adequately balance the interests of the contractor and the Government. Accordingly, before entering into any license negotiations, it is crucial that both parties have clearly identified their core requirements, needs, and objectives. For DoD, this requires that IP considerations have been fully integrated into the acquisition plan (see Core Principle 1 and Chapter 3).

When negotiating a special license, carefully select the starting point or template for the license agreement. There is no need to reinvent the wheel. Consider the following:

- ◆ If the negotiation involves commercial technologies, consider starting with the license agreement that is customarily offered to the public.

- ◆ If the negotiation involves noncommercial technologies, consider starting with the standard DFARS license that most closely parallels the relative funding of the parties.

- ◆ For development primarily funded at private expense, start with limited or restricted rights and add the additional rights the Government needs.

- ◆ For development primarily funded at Government expense, start with GPR and add limitations to preserve additional rights for the contractor-developer.

After selecting the appropriate starting point, there are several general principles to keep in mind when crafting specialized provisions:

- ◆ The Government cannot accept less than limited rights in noncommercial technical data, the standard "7015 rights" in commercial technical data, or restricted rights in noncommercial computer software (unless a waiver is obtained).

- ◆ The license should clearly set forth the data/software covered by the license, by identifying specific deliverables or establishing well-defined classes, categories, or types of deliverables; and the license should clearly set forth the specific rights granted to the Government, by enumerating all restrictions on the Government's ability to use, reproduce, modify, release, perform, display, and disclose the licensed materials, and authorize others to engage in those activities.

- ◆ The Government's license should be royalty-free (meaning that the license fee is included in the contract price), worldwide, irrevocable, and nonexclusive.

Specific examples and suggestions for special license provisions are discussed in Chapter 4, Issue Category 3.

MARKINGS AND RESTRICTIVE LEGENDS

Rights and obligations concerning restrictive markings or notices play a central role in many forms of IP. Restrictive markings are either required or permitted on all forms of technical data or computer software that is to be delivered to DoD. The specific format and content of these markings depends on whether the data or software is noncommercial or commercial.

Restrictive Markings on Noncommercial Data and Software

Restrictive markings are required for all noncommercial technical data and computer software being delivered with less-than-unlimited rights. The DFARS establishes specific procedures governing the placement of restrictive markings on deliverables, storage media, and transmittal documents. In addition, there are only six types of legends that are authorized under the clauses:

- A notice of copyright under 17 U.S.C. 401 or 402,

- The GPR legend,

- The limited-rights legend,

- The restricted-rights legend,

- The special-license-rights legend, and

- Pre-existing markings authorized under a previous Government contract.

The DFARS clauses specify the precise wording of the legends. Any alterations of the prescribed content or format result in the marking being considered "nonconforming."

Restrictive Markings on Commercial Data and Software

For commercial technical data and computer software the rules are more flexible, following best commercial practices. For commercial technical data, there is no prescribed legend, but DFARS 252.227-7015(d) provides that there will be no liability for the release or disclosure of technical data that is not marked to indicate that the data is subject to restrictions. The issue of markings on commercial computer software is not addressed in the DFARS, although it is customary in the commercial marketplace to mark software with appropriate legends (e.g., copyright notices).

SUMMARY

The IP law and its application to Government contracting is complex, and some people spend their entire careers interpreting only one small aspect of it. Inventions and creative works are developed at what seems to be a daily rate, so IP increasingly is a significant asset to corporations and its protection is at the forefront of every corporate philosophy. Stock market analysts, venture capitalists, and investment bankers base a large part of their valuation of a company on its IP and the company's ability to leverage new products and profits from that IP. This is largely based upon a review of the company's contracts and an assessment of how "diluted" the value of the company's IP is due to transfers, assignments, or licenses of IP to other parties. As the Government participates more and more in the commercial community and tries to act more like a commercial entity in its dealings with the civilian marketplace, the Government will have to assume a more commercial mindset when acquiring IP rights.

Flexibility and collaboration will be the hallmarks of future Government/industry research and development (R&D) agreements. It is, therefore, in the Government's best interest to understand and, when possible and appropriate, accommodate industry's concerns for protecting its IP. Only in this way will the Government be able to tap into the billions of dollars worth of R&D, cutting-edge technologies, and state-of-the-art commercial products available from commercial companies and the commercial divisions of traditional Defense companies.

TABLES

The following tables are applicable to Chapter 2:

- Table 2.1: The Most Common Types of Intellectual Property Protection,

- Table 2.2: Rights in Noncommercial Computer Software (CS) and Technical Data (TD) Covering Noncommercial Items, and

- Table 2.3: Rights in Commercial Computer Software (CS) and Technical Data (TD) Covering Commercial Items.

Table 2-1. The Most Common Types of Intellectual Property Protection
(See Appendix B for detailed discussion)

Type of IP Protection	Protectable Subject Matter	Nature of Protection/Rights Granted to the IP Owner	Requirements for Protection	Remedies Available	Duration of Protection	Statutory Basis	DoD-Specific Statutes/Regs
Patents[1]	Processes, machines, articles of manufacture, and compositions of matter.	Right to exclude others from making, using, selling, or importing the invention; sometimes referred to as the right to exclude others from "practicing" the invention.	Application filed in U.S. Patent & Trademark Office; invention must be new, useful, and non-obvious.	Money damages, and injunction.[2]	20 years from application date.	Title 35 U.S.C.; 28 U.S.C. 1498(a).	FAR 27.1 to 27.3 and related clauses; DFARS 227.3 and 227.70, and related clauses.
Copyrights	Original, creative works fixed in a tangible medium of expression (e.g., literary, musical, or audiovisual works; computer programs).	Exclusive right to (1) copy; (2) modify;[3] (3) perform; (4) display; and (5) distribute copies of the copyrighted work. No protection against independent creation of similar works, or against certain "fair uses."	Automatic when fixed in a tangible medium; added remedies for registration and notice.	Money damages (actual or statutory)[2], injunction, and criminal sanctions.[4]	Life of the author plus 70 years.	Title 17 U.S.C.; 28 U.S.C. 1498(b).	10 U.S.C. 2320 and 2321; DFARS Subparts 227.71 and 227.72, and related clauses.
Trade Secrets	Any information having commercial value by being kept secret (e.g., technical, business, or financial information)	Right to control the disclosure and use of the information through contracts or nondisclosure agreements; protection against theft or misappropriation of that information, but not from independent creation or discovery by another party.	Must take reasonable steps to safeguard the information from disclosure; reasonableness depends on the value of the information.	Money damages, injunction, and criminal sanctions.[4]	Potentially unlimited, as long as remains secret.	18 U.S.C. 1905; 18 U.S.C. 1831-39; various state laws.	10 U.S.C. 2320 and 2321; DFARS Subparts 227.71 and 227.72, and related clauses.
Trademarks and Service Marks	Distinctive words, phrases, or symbols that identify the source of goods or services.	Protection from confusingly similar marks, deception, and unfair competition in the marketing of goods and services.	Automatic upon use in commerce; added remedies for registration and notice.	Money damages, injunction, and criminal sanctions.[4]	Federal registration can be renewed every 10 years.	Title 15 U.S.C.; various state laws.	None; although a new draft FAR subpart is under development.

Notes :

1. Information provided here for "utility" patents—the type most common in DoD acquisitions ; see Appendix B for details on "plant" patents and "design" patents.
2. There is no injunctive relief available against the Government for patent or copyright infringement; see 28 U.S.C. 1498(a) and (b).
3. This right is more formally called the right to create a "derivative work" by modifying an existing copyrighted work.
4. Although private individuals cannot enforce criminal penalties, violations of criminal statutes may be reported to the appropriate authorities.

Table 2-2. Rights[1] in Noncommercial Computer Software (CS) and Technical Data (TD) Covering Noncommercial Items

Rights Category[2]	Applicable to TD or CS?	Criteria for Applying Rights Category	Permitted Uses within Government	Permitted Uses outside Government[3]
Unlimited Rights (UR)	Both TD and CS	Development exclusively at Government expense[4], also any deliverable of certain types—regardless of funding.[5]	Unlimited; no restrictions.	Unlimited; no restrictions.
Government Purpose Rights (GPR)	Both TD and CS	Development with mixed funding.[4]	Unlimited; no restrictions.	Only for "Government purposes", no commercial use.
Limited Rights (LR)	TD only	Development exclusively at private expense.[4]	Unlimited, except may not be used for manufacture.	Emergency repair/overhaul; evaluation by foreign government.
Restricted Rights (RR)	CS only	Development[1] exclusively at private expense.	Only one computer at a time; minimum backup copies; modification.	Emergency repair/overhaul; certain service/maintenance contracts.
Prior Government Rights	Both TD and CS	Whenever Government has previously acquired rights in the deliverable TD/CS	Same as under the previous contract.	
Specifically Negotiated License Rights (SNLR)	Both TD and CS	Mutual agreement of the parties; use whenever the standard rights categories do not meet both parties' needs	As negotiated by the parties; however, must not be less than LR in TD, and must not be less than RR in CS.[6]	

Notes:

1. _Critical Need to Specify Deliverables_. The standard clauses address rights but do *not* include delivery requirements. The contract must explicitly specify the content, format, and delivery medium for all IP deliverables that are necessary to meet DoD's needs. For CS, it is critical to specify requirements for both the executable code and the source code.

2. _Mandatory Listing Requirements_. All TD and CS to be delivered with less than UR *must* be identified in a list attached to the contract. Pre-award listing requirements are specified at DFARS 252.227-7017; post-award requirements are at DFARS 252.227-7013(e) and -7014(e).

3. _Release Procedures/Restrictions_. All authorized third-party recipients of TD/CS with other than UR must either sign the standard NDA from DFARS 227.7103-7 or receive the TD/CS under a contract containing DFARS 252.227-7025. Additional notice requirements exist for releases of LR data or RR software.

4. _Source of Development Funding—at the "Lowest Practicable Level."_ For TD, the determination is based on the funding for the development of the item, component, or process (ICP) to which that data pertains (vice the development of the technical data itself). For CS, the determination is based on the source of funding for that software. If the ICP or software is developed with mixed funding, the default GPR license may be inequitable if the Government has funded only a small portion of the overall development costs. This imbalance is resolved by determining the source of funding at "lowest practicable level": the deliverable ICP or software is divided into segregable components (e.g., sub-elements of ICPs, or sub-routines of CS), and the funding determination is made for each of the components individually. For TD, see DFARS 227.7103-4(b) and 252.227-7013(a)(6)-(9); for CS, see DFARS 227.7203-4(b) and 252.227-7014(a)(6)-(9).

5. _Unlimited Rights—Regardless of Funding Source._ Paragraph (b)(1) of the DFARS 252.227-7013 and -7014 clauses establish numerous categories for which the Government is entitled to receive UR, regardless of which party funded the development of the underlying technology. For example, "form, fit, and function" data; or data/software that is publicly available without restrictions. See 10 U.S.C. 2320(a)(2)(C).

6. _Minimum Rights._ For TD, the minimum rights are established by statute (10 U.S.C. 2320) and are nonnegotiable. For CS, the minimum rights are based solely on the DFARS, for which the parties could seek a deviation in circumstances in which DoD's requirements can be satisfied with less than RR.

Table 2-3. Rights[1,2] in Commercial Computer Software[3,4] (CS) and Technical Data (TD) Covering Commercial Items[3,4]

Rights Category[5]	Applicable to TD or CS?	Criteria for Applying Rights Category	Permitted Uses within Government	Permitted Uses outside Government
Unlimited Rights (UR)	TD only	Any TD of certain specified types or classes, regardless of commercial status.[6]	Unlimited; no restrictions.	
Standard DFARS "7015" Rights	TD only	Default rights category for all TD covering commercial items except those qualifying for UR as stated above.	Unlimited, except may not be used for manufacture.	Only for emergency repair and overhaul.
Standard Commercial License	CS only	Default rights category for all commercial CS.	As specified in the license customarily offered to the public; DoD must negotiate for any specialized needs.	As specified in the license customarily offered to the public, as long as the
Specifically Negotiated License Rights (SNLR)	Both TD and CS	Mutual agreement of the parties; should be used whenever the standard rights do not meet both parties' needs.	As negotiated by the parties; however, by statute, the Government cannot accept less than the minimum standard 7015 rights in TD.[7]	

Notes:

1. <u>Critical Impact on IP Delivery Requirements</u>. DoD policy is to acquire, in addition to lesser rights, only those IP deliverables that are customarily offered to the public. In many cases this will be substantially different (e.g., less detailed TD; no source code for CS) than the deliverables DoD typically receives for noncommercial TD or CS. DoD must specifically negotiate for any additional IP deliverables that it requires.

2. <u>Key: Early Identification of Commercial Technologies</u>. Because both the IP deliverables and the license rights are significantly affected when acquiring commercial technologies, it is critical to identify how these issues affect the acquisition strategy early in the acquisition process.

3. <u>Definitions</u>. "Commercial item" is defined at FAR 2.101 (and 52.202-1), and "commercial computer software" is defined in DFARS 252.227-7014(a)(1).

4. <u>Adapting/Modifying Commercial Items</u>. Commercial items may be modified to meet DoD's requirements without losing their commercial status, as long as the adaptations qualify as "minor modifications" or modifications "of a type customarily available in the commercial marketplace." See FAR 2.101(c), and DFARS 252.227-7014(a)(1) and (12).

5. <u>DFARS Rights versus Standard Commercial Licenses</u>. Rights in TD covering commercial items are specified at DFARS 252.227-7015; the default rights are similar to limited rights that apply to noncommercial TD. There is no clause covering commercial CS; DoD takes the rights customarily offered to the public (often a "shrink-wrap" or "click-wrap" license) unless those rights do not meet DoD's minimum needs or violate Federal procurement law. In all cases, a copy of the standard commercial license agreement or any SNLR must be attached to the contract.

6. <u>Unlimited Rights—Regardless of Commercial Status</u>. DFARS 252.227-7015(b)(1) lists numerous categories of TD for which the Government is entitled to receive UR—regardless of the commercial status or source of funding for the technology. For example, "form, fit, and function" data or data/software that is publicly available without restrictions. The categories are based on 10 U.S.C. 2320(a)(2)(C).

7. <u>Minimum Rights</u>. For TD, the minimum rights are established by statute (10 U.S.C. 2320) and are nonnegotiable.

Chapter 3
Acquisition Planning

Good acquisition planning, including market research, begins with a review and complete understanding of the requirements. Only through understanding the real program requirements can a contracting officer anticipate the valid Government interests in IP. This understanding can begin to shape the procurement process in order to achieve the maximum participation of commercial sources and maintain appropriately designed program competition. Early planning and market research will best enable the contracting officer to assess the environment and requirements, incorporate this knowledge into the acquisition strategy, and make the best business deal for the Government. Acquisition planning continues throughout the life of the contractual instrument and program cycles. Paying constant attention to postaward issues and planning for their resolution are as important as initial contract placement planning. This is particularly true in a rapidly changing technology area.

Remember, many commercial technologies are attractive solutions to DoD's performance and affordability needs. In most cases, DoD has not invested heavily in development costs in these technologies. Wider markets for the commercial items ensure that DoD's portion of the development costs is minimized. IP is intangible property and is an asset that may be used and built upon repeatedly; therefore, the IP owner is able to recoup costs and profit from multiple transactions. Each transaction thus bears only a fraction of the development cost. The greater the number of transactions, the lower the shared cost per transaction. Thus, both parties benefit as the market base (i.e., the number of transactions) grows. In addition, worldwide commercial market pressures on these technologies will help ensure long-term competition in price, technical support, and technology upgrades.

POLICY CHANGES

Much has changed in the acquisition environment in recent years. Laws have been enacted, policy changes have been articulated, and many programs now pursue substantively different strategies that embrace technology and meet warfighter needs faster, better, and cheaper. These changes have been driven by some of the following objectives:

◆ Stay "closer" to technological advances in the commercial sector and have access to firms performing at the cutting edges of advanced technologies.

◆ Define requirements in terms of performance or outcomes rather than through detailed design specifications.

- Attract commercial firms and their advancing technology to the Government marketplace with the use of other transaction authority or FAR Part 12 procedures.

- Match the system development cycle to the technology turnover cycle to achieve earlier technology insertion and improvement upgrades.

- Increase reliance on contractor logistics support, including just-in-time supply support, to reduce the Defense inventory infrastructure.

- Recognize that the Defense-unique marketplace is not large enough to support a unique industrial base and infrastructure.

Contracting officers must work very closely with the acquisition team to sort out many of the critical questions that are addressed by these objectives and that influence commercial industry involvement. The team must be sure that requirements and strategies embedded in the various aspects of the solicitation do not inadvertently limit the Department's options in accessing vital technology and commercial solutions available from companies that heretofore have refused to do business under historical IP approaches. Market research and long-term planning are the best weapons to combat this dilemma.

MARKET RESEARCH

"Market research," as used here, is the process of identifying appropriate commercial technologies to meet Government needs. The following IP issues should be explored during market research:

- What is the maturity level of relevant commercial technologies?

- Can existing technologies be adapted for DoD requirements?

- For each technology, what are the standard commercial approaches to the nature and type of data to be furnished to commercial end-users, and what license rights are typically provided to end-users (vice co-developers)?

- What is the business tradeoff between buying established technology from multiple competitive sources and buying state-of-the-art technology that requires alternative approaches to achieving competitive market pricing?

- To what extent will the standard data rights and patent clauses discourage vitally needed firms from participating?

- What is the pace of technology? (For example, a company whose software technology turns over every year or so is unlikely to pursue a patent; a trade secret is the more likely IP route in this situation.)

♦ What is the Government's relative position (e.g., a small or large buyer) in this market?

♦ Would a company acquire the same IP rights in a similar situation?

If market research reveals that a practice or particular strategy is in the best interest of the Government and is not specifically addressed in the regulations, nor prohibited by law or executive order, the Government team can assume it is not prohibited and pursue it, with appropriate legal counsel, if it creates a win-win scenario.

LONG-TERM PLANNING

Acquisition planners should consider both the instant project requirements and any expected production and/or support follow-on activity required. If no future buys are planned or if maintenance and support will be done through exercising negotiated warranties, the need for technical data and other IP is greatly reduced. If the developer is embracing the concept of contractor logistics support, the need for technical data downstream may be obviated and may thereby remove that IP barrier from the procurement. If, on the other hand, organic maintenance capability is required at some level, new assumptions should be considered. For example, planning for downstream competitions on subsystems based on form, fit, and function requirements, will reduce the need for technical data that would form the basis for a reprocurement of precisely the same item.

It is essential that the acquisition team apply good business sense when considering the balance of the Government's and industry's needs for IP rights. For example, what good is done if highly restrictive data rights and patent clauses are used that may only discourage vitally needed technology firms from participating? Competition would be reduced and the key technology leaders in a particular field may not participate. The Government's interests can be best protected by changing the IP-affected clauses as needed to obtain broader participation for the technological leaders to meet the Defense need.

Early and continued communication among all disciplines of the team, including program, contracting, logistics, and legal counsel, will enhance the likelihood of a successful program and ensure early appropriate focus on the IP issues. Involving commercial industry in the planning process also will provide the necessary commercial input that can help shape the acquisition strategy and program plan.

Part of the planning process is to determine where that technical "trade space" is and how potential commercial technologies can meet the need. One way to achieve this determination is through effective market research. Another widely used approach is the issuance of sources sought and draft solicitations. These contacts should be part of the plan as a way to make potential sources aware of the program and to help determine whether the draft solicitation has restrictive minimum technical or IP requirements that may preclude commercial companies' involvement.

The contracting officer must embrace the responsibility to ensure the IP terms and conditions negotiated are appropriate for the particular project. The contracting officer must understand the short- and long-term implications of his or her position, on commercial industry, including the use of standard clauses that may result in limiting competition from the commercial sector. Commercial firms do not necessarily know of or understand the clauses, or recognize that they are negotiable. When a procurement action is very dependent upon new or emerging technology, a good strategy is to begin by including only the minimum clauses, recognizing that others can be added through negotiations if necessary. Further, an affirmative statement regarding DoD's approach to IP, asking for companies to indicate alternative approaches if necessary to secure commercial technology, could be included in the solicitation. Contracting officers should refer to the core IP principles (set forth in Chapter 1) in creating the acquisition strategy.

COMPETITION

The need for competition has stimulated much of the desire to acquire technical data and assert patent rights. In the past, to ensure that the prices for spare parts for maintenance were fair, programs would acquire technical data packages (e.g., detailed design drawings, manufacturing data, and source code). The technical data packages would be used for the follow-on competitive reprocurement of spares, year after year, to support fielded systems maintained by the military services and stockpiled by the Defense Logistics Agency and military depots. However, in recent years, this type of competition strategy has become obsolete; DoD has moved instead from form, fit, and function specifications to contractor logistics support strategies and just-in-time inventory spares/parts supply. With this in mind, contracting officers and program managers should look to satisfy competition requirements through alternative strategies such as

- long-term initial competitive contracts,

- cycling technical insertion in shorter increments by using form, fit, and function specifications that enable new entrants; and

- dissimilar competition (see DoD Directives 5000.1 and 5000.2).

Another area of competition that sometimes impacts the perceived need for IP occurs when the Government outsources maintenance operations. While the tendency of viable competitors is to ask for technical data to perform such functions, alternative strategies should be pursued if at all possible. For example, even if the Government accomplished maintenance and refurbishments using original design data, outsourcing to industry may create an opportunity for the Government to pursue performance-based approaches. This may not only obviate the need for data, but also improve quality and reduce cost.

DELIVERABLE REQUIREMENTS

When planning deliverable requirements, it is critical to determine whether the technology being acquired qualifies as a "commercial item"[1] or as "commercial computer software."[2] Not only is there a statutory preference for commercial items, but this determination may have a significant impact on the both the nature of the deliverable and the associated license rights.

Many commercial technologies require some adaptation to meet DoD's requirements. A frequently made mistake is presuming that modification of the commercial technology causes that item to lose its status as a commercial item. The definitions for commercial items and commercial computer software both permit the item/software in question to undergo "minor modifications" or modifications "of a type customarily available in the commercial marketplace" and still qualify under the respective definitions.

SUMMARY

One of the simplest and yet most important aspects of acquiring IP is identifying the critical issues prior to contract award. Taking the steps discussed above to identify and resolve key IP issues early will benefit all parties, by

◆ ensuring the contractors' ability to preserve valuable IP interests by asserting restrictions on trade secret information,

◆ facilitating source selection by identifying IP-based restrictions that may impact the overall life-cycle cost of competing technologies,

◆ facilitating structured negotiations by ensuring that the parties are fully aware of the critical IP issues, and

◆ providing convenient methods for incorporating the results of IP negotiations into the contract.

---

[1] "Commercial item" is defined at FAR 2.101 (and 52.202-1).

[2] "Commercial computer software" is defined at DFARS 252.227-7014(a)(1).

Chapter 4
Issues and Solutions

To meet the ultimate objectives of the Department, contracting officers must be better equipped to handle the complex and myriad issues that may arise under IP discussions. This chapter offers potential solutions to often difficult IP challenges posed by various FAR and DFARS clauses. The issues are grouped in the following seven categories:

1. Application of Intellectual Property Clauses

2. Patent Rights—Retention by the Contractor (FAR 52.227-11 and–12)

3. Rights in Technical Data—Noncommercial Items (DFARS 252-227-7013) and Rights in Noncommercial Computer Software and Noncommercial Computer Software Documentation (DFARS 252.227-7014)

4. Technical Data—Commercial Items (DFARS 252.227-7015)

5. Royalty Information (FAR 52.227-6)

6. Disclosure of Information (DFARS 252.204-7000)

7. Deferred Delivery of Technical Data or Computer Software (DFARS 252.227-7026), Deferred Ordering of Technical Data or Computer Software (DFARS 252.227-7027), and Additional Data Requirements (FAR 52.227-16)

Each issue is treated in sections below that describe the related clause, highlight industry concerns, summarize the Government's viewpoint, and finally—and most importantly—provide potential solutions.

The contracting officer should consider typical FAR and DFARS procedures and clauses for IP, as well as common commercial business practices, and ultimately negotiate clauses that appropriately reflect the risk to be undertaken by all parties on their particular contract. Reflecting upon the core IP principles described in Chapter 1 also will help in navigating through these murky waters. Regardless of their approach, contracting officers should, of course, consult with their local general counsel and, if available, IP attorneys. In the end they should negotiate appropriate arrangements that will meet the Government's vital interests. Appendix G provides a resource list of Department IP attorneys who can assist in providing advice in these matters.

ISSUE CATEGORY 1: APPLICATION OF INTELLECTUAL PROPERTY CLAUSES

Issue 1-A: Application of the Patent Clauses

Clause

FAR 52.227-12 is required for contracts where the effort is for experimental, research, or developmental work with large, for-profit business entities. (FAR 52.227-11 is required for contracts for such work with small businesses and non-profit organizations.)

While these clauses are prescribed for use in research, experimental, and developmental contracts, they are being found in other type of contracts. It is sometimes difficult to determine whether a particular contract qualifies under these criteria.

Industry Concern

In general, industry prefers not to have these clauses in its contracts because of the various rights, restrictions, and requirements that are treated later in this chapter. In addition, because the patent rights clauses do not account for a company's financial investment in creating the IP, the clauses could inhibit the company's ability to secure private funding from venture capitalists who view these clauses as an unnecessary risk.

Government Viewpoint

The purposes of these clauses are to ensure that inventions developed under Government funding are properly utilized to benefit the public and to treat subcontractors fairly. The Government receives license rights to use the IP for Government purposes.

Solution

Contracting officers should not use these clauses unless they are clearly applicable. Involvement of the acquisition team, including legal counsel, may be required to determine applicability. To determine whether the clauses are required, the emphasis should be placed on the nature of the work being done, not necessarily on the source of development funding (i.e., Government versus private), the "color of money" (e.g., research funds), or the phase of the system being acquired (e.g., engineering and manufacturing development). For example, contractors working on proposed new computer interfaces may be funded with research funds, but the nature of the work is not experimental, developmental, or research oriented. This is not to say that the Government might not acquire unlimited rights in the resulting technical data or computer software, but research is not expected and therefore the patent clause would be inapplicable. As another example, if the contract is for services that modify a commercial item or adapt a commercial technology to meet the Government's need, the contract need not include the patent clause. This is true even if the modification has never been done before, provided the modification is a "minor modification" or a modification customarily performed in the commercial marketplace.

The activity of modifying a commercial item for DoD use may not necessarily fall within the definition of "development work." The key to this judgment is whether the modification effort is routine and does not necessitate significant engineering or redesign effort. If so, it is a modification—not experimental or research—and therefore does not require the FAR clause. In contrast, major engineering efforts fall in the realm of "development work." Involving legal counsel is important if the distinction in these two categories becomes an issue.

Issue 1-B: Previously Developed Intellectual Property

Clauses

The patent, technical data, and computer software clauses are drafted to cover a broad range of contracting and technology-development scenarios. Accordingly, the standard rights categories established by these clauses may not always allocate rights in a manner that most effectively satisfies the needs of all parties. This problem is most evident when the contract work involves a significant amount of "background IP" (i.e., IP developed at private expense prior to, or outside, the Government contract), which must be modified to meet Government needs. Without certain negotiated agreements, this background IP may be significantly affected by the standard rights provided in the clauses.

Industry Concern

Previously developed trade secrets may have to be divulged under the mandatory disclosure and filing requirements of the standard patent rights clauses. Similarly, when privately funded background IP is modified at Government expense, the standard technical data and software rights clauses treat the development as "mixed funding." This results in the Government receiving a broad GPR license that does not adequately account for the significant private investment made previously.

Government Viewpoint

The Government historically has maintained the position that the Government acquires license rights in contract results obtained whenever the Government funds a portion of the development. The patent rights clauses are intended to reach only those inventions that are created under a Government contract. The noncommercial technical data and computer software clauses allocate rights based on which party funded the development of the technology. For commercial technical data, the Government receives a very restrictive license, and for commercial computer software, the Government typically receives only the standard commercial license rights.

Solution

The Government needs to recognize that that a contractor's background IP is vital to that company's commercial success and business interests. Protecting these rights will encourage further commercial participation and support companies' efforts to obtain additional capital for further research investment.

To help identify and protect background IP, offerors and contracting officers must be firm in requiring a list of proprietary technologies up front in the proposal, including noncommercial data/software, commercial data/software, and if possible, background inventions and other relevant IP. While the source selection may be affected if the Government's acquisition plan includes future competitive phases (*e.g.*, production, procurement of spares, life-cycle support, or upgrade), the contracting officer and the offeror must have a full understanding of the scope of the IP or data discussions. In addition, during the post-award period, the contracting officer should permit the contractor to modify the listing reasonably.

DoD's way of handling a contractor's previously developed, copyrighted material, proprietary data, and trade secrets is through the application of restrictive legends on deliverable data. The contractor can protect delivered data through the assertion of limited/restricted rights by including the requisite legends. However, note that restrictive legends are permitted only if the data has been identified on the required listing of asserted restrictions.

The patent rights clauses grant the Government rights only if the invention is either conceived or first actually reduced to practice during contract performance. Thus, if the contractor can demonstrate that an invention falls outside of the relevant contract—or any other Federal contract—the Government will not acquire any patent rights. In addition, defining the research scope of work carefully and specifically will clarify the effort and make it easier to determine what IP was developed prior to, or outside, the scope of the contract work. See Issue Category 2, Patent Rights—Retention by Contractor, for additional discussion of how the disclosure and filing requirements impact background IP.

When background IP will be incorporated into technical data or computer software delivered under the contract, the critical first step is to determine whether the technology is commercial or noncommercial:

- ◆ For technical data pertaining to commercial items, the standard rights granted to the Government are very restrictive—similar to limited rights in noncommercial technical data. For commercial computer software, the Government receives only the standard commercial license. In each case, DoD must negotiate for any specialized needs. As stated earlier, commercial technologies can be adapted to DoD's needs without losing their commercial status.

◆ The noncommercial technical data and computer software rights clauses allocate rights based on determining whose funding supported the effort to create the IP. The concepts of Government-funded, private-expense, or co-funded (or cost-shared) efforts are critical to the negotiation of these rights. The contractor should assert limited rights protection in technical data, and restricted rights protection for computer software, that pertain to technologies developed exclusively at private expense. The important issue here is whether the contractor—as opposed to the Government—paid for part of the development of the item, component, or process shown in the data. The current regulations at DFARS 252.227-7103(a)(7) provide: " 'developed exclusively at private expense' means development was accomplished entirely with costs charged to indirect cost pools, costs not allocated to a Government contract, or any combination thereof."

Issue 1-C: Alternatives for Acquiring Commercial Research Services

Clauses and Procurement Method

The Government is having difficulty in attracting truly commercial business to research Government problems, whether in research programs or in weapons systems development programs. This is largely due to the use of traditional IP clauses and procurement methods.

Industry Concern

In the commercial R&D business, companies view the scientist's or engineer's time as a scarce resource. Given the options to use this resource to generate economic wealth (by retaining all of the IP rights) or to sell this resource for a fee (which often involves selling or sharing the resulting IP rights), most firms will select the first. This means many commercial companies may refuse to do business with the Government because they believe that they will be forced to give up their IP rights under a traditional Government contract.

Government Viewpoint

Alternatives to traditional Government contracts are available. Other transaction authority is flexible and provides the Department the opportunity to streamline the acquisition process, facilitate the development of contractor strategic relationships, take advantage of innovative or commercial business practices, and attract companies that traditionally do not do business with the government. Because "other transactions" are not subject to the FAR and most procurement statutes, this method can be particularly attractive to new contractors that otherwise would be averse to Government contracting. FAR Part 12, Acquisition of Commercial

Items, was created, based on the Federal Acquisition Streamlining Act,[1] to promote commercial item buying and enhance the opportunities for attracting commercial industry to the Government marketplace. Applying the streamlined procedures of FAR Part 12 to the acquisition of commercial services—even research-related services—furthers those objectives. Additionally, recent legislative language provides incentives for using FAR Part 12 when buying performance-based services.[2]

Solution

Use other transactions for prototype agreements (transactions other than procurement contracts, cooperative agreements, or grants) when acquiring commercial R&D services. For research-related services (e.g., testing or lab services that may have a commercial market), the acquisition team should investigate the use of FAR Part 12. The contracting officer acquires commercial services for a particular application or purpose, and the contractor receives IP rights to all other applications of that technology. The use of FAR Part 12 allows the contracting officer to negotiate clauses, including those associated with IP rights, that are consistent with demonstrated commercial practices. It should be noted that, under FAR Part 12, a fixed-price contract is required. Under such a research-related services contract, the structure would need to permit milestone-type achievements and payments, without placing undue risk on the contractor.

ISSUE CATEGORY 2: PATENT RIGHTS—RETENTION BY THE CONTRACTOR (FAR 52.227-11 AND -12)

Regarding large, for-profit businesses, the only provisions of the Patent Rights—Retention by the Contractor (Long Form) clause that are statutory and cannot be waived or modified are the Government-purpose license and "march-in rights."[3] Therefore, the contracting officer can obtain a FAR deviation modifying the FAR 52.227-12 patent rights clause for all other issues arising under this clause.

Issue 2-A: Conceived or First Actually Reduced to Practice

Clauses

These clauses are applicable to subject inventions either conceived or first actually reduced to practice under the contract. "Conceived" refers to a mental act of developing the idea for a fully functional invention. For the purposes of Government contract law and proof in a court of law, the conception of the idea must be

---

[1] Federal Acquisition Streamlining Act of 1994, Public Law 103-355.

[2] Fiscal Year 2001 Defense Authorization Act, Public Law 106-398 Section 821, 106th Cong., 2nd sess., H.R. 4205, 30 October 2000.

[3] 35 U.S.C. 210(c), Patent Rights in Inventions Made with Federal Assistance—Precedence of Chapter.

documented (e.g., making a drawing of the invention). "First actually reduced to practice" occurs when an invention has been embodied in some physical form, which is used to demonstrate its workability. Workability requires that the physical embodiment be tested, unless it is so simple that no tests are necessary. Workability may be tested in the laboratory in the intended environments. Yet, in general, the courts have not considered simulation to be "actual" reduction to practice.

Industry Concern

Industry objects to this aspect of the clauses because companies may have conceived the invention outside of any Government contract. They may have invested heavily in background technology, including sophisticated computer simulations or modeling, and yet a potentially small Government contract could jeopardize their return merely because they might first "actually" or physically reduce the invention to practice under the contract. Further, a patent may already have been awarded based on constructive reduction to practice (perhaps through simulation) and still may be at risk because it may not have been actually reduced to practice until performance under the Government contract. As a result of this concern, industry may refuse the Government contract.

Government Viewpoint

If the Government's funding permitted the first actual reduction to practice, then the Government should not have to pay royalties for its use of the patent. However, the interpretation and application of the standard for actual reduction to practice must take into account the current best practices and technical realities concerning simulation and modeling.

Solution

The parties should carefully craft the statement of work to preclude the actual reduction to practice of previously conceived inventions from occurring under, and being charged to, the Government contract. The contractor also should be sure to advise the Government of work conducted prior to the award of the contract and any pending patents or patents awarded based on constructive reduction to practice. The contracting officer could add a special provision to the contract that articulates the type of prior or continuing work that will be excluded from any future claims for IP rights.

It may be cost-prohibitive for the contractor to actually reduce the invention to practice at its own expense, opting instead for some type of simulation to prove workability of the invention. In fact, some of today's most complex technological creations (e.g., aircraft and submarines) are designed, simulated, and tested almost entirely on computer. Computer-aided design, modeling, and manufacturing software is so advanced that complex systems can be "virtually" reduced to practice with such accuracy and reliability that they may qualify as having been actually reduced to practice. Under this circumstance, the contracting officer could include a special provision that actual reduction to practice could include simulation if the technology is sufficiently mature to reasonably ensure workability. While the courts historically have not supported simulation as evidence of workability, this does not preclude the parties from that agreement if the case is made.

Issue 2-B: Disclosure and Filing Requirements

Clauses

By statute, small businesses and non-profit businesses must, after the election of title, file a patent application within a reasonable time after the invention becomes known to the contractor personnel who are responsible for the administration of patent matters. By regulation, this same requirement applies to large, for-profit businesses. The clauses require this application to be filed within one year of title-election unless a certain event (i.e., prior publication, public use, or "on sale") has occurred, in which case the application must be made within one year from that event. If the contractor, large or small, fails to meet this requirement, the Government may take title to the invention and file a patent application on its own behalf.[4]

Industry Concern

Some issues in Government contracts regarding trade secrets are beginning to arise for several reasons:

- ◆ The Government is increasingly entering mixed-funding agreements, where a private party funds a portion of the work;

- ◆ The Government is no longer the biggest customer—or even a major customer—for most companies, who feel losing their trade secret rights—thus affecting their commercial business—is not worth the relatively small Federal Government revenue;

- ◆ Commercial companies may prefer to maintain proprietary information associated with an invention as a trade secret in lieu of filing a patent; and

- ◆ Disclosure of the subject invention potentially compromises the ability for a company to maintain certain trade secrets.

The time period to file a patent application after reporting an invention is considered by industry to be too short. Some companies do not patent any inventions, preferring instead to keep them as trade secrets. Trade secret protection often is used for process inventions and similar inventions where the use of the invention is not obvious. If a company cannot tell whether a potential infringer is using a

---

[4] 35 U.S.C. 202 (c)3, Patent Rights in Inventions Made with Federal Assistance—Disposition of Rights.

patented invention (as in the case of process patents), it cannot enforce its rights under patent law. Therefore it may choose to maintain the invention as a trade secret.

In other cases, when filing a patent application, the contractor may be required to disclose background trade secrets of the technology due to the "best mode" requirement under U.S. patent law. The background information may be the contractor's previously developed trade secrets, which would be destroyed by disclosing that information as part of the patent application. This concern is exacerbated by new laws permitting public disclosure of patent applications prior to patent issuance.

Government Viewpoint

The time frames are established by regulation to discipline the process so that the commercialization of Government-funded inventions will take place and to ensure that patent protection is not prohibited due to a statutory bar.

Solution

FAR 52.227-12(c)(4) allows the contractor to request an extension of time to file a patent application, which the agency may grant at its discretion, as long as the filing occurs prior to the end of the "statutory bar" period (i.e., one year after any publication, public use, or public sale). The contractor should take advantage of this opportunity. Pre-contract approval of a time extension also is possible. In the case where the company desires to maintain the invention as a trade secret, the contracting officer could extend the time required for the contractor to disclose the invention to Government. That extension could be based upon simply increasing the period of time or identifying the achievement of a specific event that allows the company to protect the trade secret long enough for business purposes.

Another approach that may be used is one similar to that followed by the National Institutes of Health (NIH) with respect to patentable biological materials, where the standard industry practice is to keep such inventions as a trade secret rather than to patent them. Under NIH procedures for handling non-election of title to patentable biological materials, the NIH agrees in advance that the contractor may keep the patentable subject invention a trade secret and the Government will not request title to the invention so long as the contractor meets certain agreed-upon terms and conditions. Similar to the NIH procedure, DoD may also agree in advance, in writing, that the contractor may keep any type of subject invention a trade secret and the Government will not request title to the invention so long as certain conditions, similar to the following, are met:

♦ The contractor will disclose the existence of the trade secret to the Government;

♦ The Government receives a nonexclusive license to practice the invention for appropriately limited Government (i.e., noncommercial) purposes;

- The contractor, assignee, or exclusive licensee, will take effective steps, within a reasonable period of time, to achieve practical application of the invention; and

- The contractor will agree that, if such steps are not taken, the Government will be allowed to license the invention.

Issue 2-C: Subcontractor Title Retention

Clauses

The Patent Rights clauses include subcontractor flow-down requirements that permit subcontractors to retain title to subject inventions made under subcontract, and establish a limited form of contract privity between the Government and subcontractor for matters relating to subject inventions.

Industry Concern

In some cases, the prime contractor may have co-funded the subcontractor's developmental efforts and thus believes it should have a right to IP developed under the subcontract.

Government Viewpoint

Defense policy is very clear that prime contractors should not use their leverage and bargaining power to gain rights in the IP of a subcontractor.

Solution

An approach that has been used by the National Aeronautics and Space Administration in appropriate cases is to obtain a FAR deviation and add a new subparagraph (g)(4) to the FAR 52.227-12 clause, Patent Rights—Retention by the Contractor, similar to the following:

"(g)(4) …In recognition of the contractor's substantial contribution of funds, facilities and/or equipment to the work performed under this contract, the Contractor is authorized, subject to the rights of the Government set forth elsewhere in this clause, to:

(i) Acquire by negotiation and mutual agreement rights to a subcontractor's subject inventions as the contractor may deem necessary to obtaining and maintaining such private support; and

(ii) Request in the event of inability to reach agreement pursuant to paragraph (g)(4)(i) of this clause, that the Government invoke exceptional circumstances as necessary pursuant to 37 CFR 401.3(a)(2) if the prospective subcontractor is a small business firm or organization or nonprofit organization, or that a FAR deviation be issued if the subcontractor is a large, for-profit business concern."

Furthermore, there is nothing to preclude a prime contractor from privately nego-tiating a separate license with the subcontractor for rights in the technology de-veloped by the subcontractor.

Finally, a contractor could seek an exceptional-circumstance determination from the agency pursuant to 35 U.S.C. 202(a)(ii) for subcontractors that are small bus i-nesses or non-profit concerns, permitting the prime contractor to obtain title in subcontractor subject inventions under the subcontract. This might occur if the prime contractor were partially funding the subcontractor's efforts. Note, how-ever, that exceptional-circumstances determinations are very difficult and time-consuming to obtain. For subcontractors that are large, for-profit businesses, a FAR waiver could also be requested, permitting the prime contractor to obtain rights in subcontractor inventions.

Issue 2-D: United States Manufacturing Requirements

Clauses

When the contractor retains title in a subject invention, under the Patent Rights clauses, the contractor is not permitted to grant *exclusive* license rights to use or sell products embodying the invention in the United States, unless the product is substantially manufactured in the United States.

Industry Concern

As companies are becoming more and more global, in order to optimize cost-effectiveness it sometimes may be necessary for the contractor or a licensee of its product to manufacture abroad. Restrictions imposed by this clause would pre-clude such action and cause the loss of profit or royalty income to the contractor, unless the product is substantially manufactured in the United States—which may not be a cost-competitive alternative. Further, U.S. manufacturers may have ex-pertise in manufacturing abroad.

Government Viewpoint

The foundation of this requirement is rooted in Buy-American-type initiatives meant to promote U.S. industry. The requirement is limited to exclusive licenses and can be waived in appropriate circumstances.

Solution

Contracting officers should emphasize that this clause applies only if the license to use or sell in the U.S. is exclusive. For example, a foreign company could be licensed to manufacture the product as long as the license was issued on a non-exclusive basis. Because the company controls who gets licensed and under what circumstances, as long as the option for a U.S. manufacturer exists, there would be no violation of the clause per se. Furthermore, the agency may waive this requirement if the owner of the patent has been unable, after reasonable efforts, to grant a license to a U.S. manufacturer, or if the patent owner can demonstrate that domestic manufacture is not commercially feasible under the circumstances. This waiver can be issued prior to entering into the contract or during contract performance, depending on the circumstances. It should be noted that the determination of "substantial" (with reference to substantial manufacture in the United States) is up to the agency's discretion. Because some companies may be concerned about the interpretation of this term, a predetermination of the definition for the specific industry, with appropriate agency counsel coordination, may be appropriate.

This requirement is not a statutory requirement for large, for-profit businesses. Therefore, a deviation may be requested to exclude this language from the FAR 52.227-12 clause, thereby rendering the U.S. manufacturing requirements moot.

Issue 2-E: Compulsory Licensing ("March-In Rights")

Clauses

When a contractor has acquired title to an invention and has not made reasonable progress in bringing it to the commercial market, the agency has the right to require the contractor to grant licenses to other applicants (e.g., potential manufacturers) under certain enumerated circumstances.[5] This compulsory licensing right of the Government is often referred to as "march-in rights." These clauses implement a major thrust of the Bayh-Dole Act, which is to ensure Government-funded research reaches the public.

Industry Concern

In spite of the fact that the Government has never taken such an action, this compulsory licensing right scares many commercial firms away from Government research business.

If invoked, compulsory-licensing rights could have serious financial consequences for the contractor. A contractor may have made substantial investment in the invention. Taking away those rights will create a liability for that contractor if the contractor is not able to achieve its return on investment. If the Government takes action to license the invention to a competitor, it will hurt the contractor's profits and the company will not be able to enjoy the exclusivity of the patent. Furthermore, the mere potential of Government compulsory licensing rights can scare off financial investment bankers, thereby making it more difficult for companies to obtain capital funding.

---

[5] 35 U.S.C. 203, Patent Rights in Inventions Made with Federal Assistance—March-In Rights; FAR 27.302(f), Patent Rights under Government Contracts—Policy.

Government Viewpoint

If the contractor has not taken effective steps to achieve a practical application of the subject invention or to meet public-use requirements specified by Federal regulations, the Government must assert this right to accomplish the objective of making Government-funded technology available to the public.

Solution

The contracting officer should emphasize to the contractor that these rights have never been exercised by DoD, and that this extreme action is authorized *only* after a determination that specific criteria are met, and *only* after providing the contractor with written notice and an opportunity to comment. Ultimately, the likelihood of this action ever being taken is very remote. The contracting officer should also make the contractor aware that a compulsory license can be disputed and an appeal made in accordance with FAR 27.304-1(g). A potential solution to this issue is to negotiate a contract provision whereby the Government would agree not to invoke compulsory licensing rights until a stated number of years (e.g., five or ten) have passed or until a specific event has occurred. This action would be considered a FAR deviation, and therefore must be approved by the head of the contracting activity.

As an additional note, it can be helpful for contracting officers and others to refrain from using the term "march-in rights," as the phrase itself sounds threatening by invoking the image of a harsh, military-type action. This image can be intimidating to the commercial firms with which DoD would like to do business.

ISSUE CATEGORY 3: RIGHTS IN TECHNICAL DATA— NONCOMMERCIAL ITEMS (DFARS 252.227-7013) AND RIGHTS IN NONCOMMERCIAL COMPUTER SOFTWARE AND NONCOMMERCIAL SOFTWARE DOCUMENTATION (DFARS 252.227-7014)

Issue 3-A: Government-Wide Licensing

Clauses

The DFARS 252.227-7013 clause (the 7013 clause) and DFARS 252.227-7014 clause (the 7014 clause) require the contractor to grant to *the Government*, in its entirety, various license rights.

Industry Concern

The rights conferred to *"the Government"* are too broad and impossible to monitor. They assert that information is poorly managed and could be transmitted to any Federal agency for any reason, without apparent control of proprietary business information. Because the Government relies heavily on support contractors and consultants, there is additional concern that the data will end up in the hands of competitors.

Government Viewpoint

One agency does not want to hamper another from using information for which the public has paid. Even though the license is Government-wide, the authorized uses of the data are significantly restricted. For example, limited rights technical data cannot be used to manufacture additional quantities of the item, and restricted rights computer software can be used only on one computer at a time and cannot be transferred to other agencies unless the transferring agency destroys its copy.

Solution

The contracting officer should carefully consider who else in the Government really needs the data and should negotiate a restricted distribution of that data. For example, data may be limited to a particular program or agency and provided on a need-to-know basis. Further, the contract could stipulate that the company's approval is required prior to submission to another Government agency. In addition, the Government must implement appropriate safeguarding measures to ensure that the Government's use of the delivered data is in strict compliance with the contractual restrictions.

Issue 3-B: Government Liability for Unauthorized Uses by Third Parties

Clauses

Under the 7013 and 7014 clauses, the contractor agrees to release the Government from any liability for the unauthorized disclosure of technical data by a third party if the Government properly released the technical data to that third party.

Industry Concern

A contractor may be reluctant to trust the Government to take adequate safeguards to protect the technical data that may be released to a third party, even though the Government is required to obtain a non-disclosure agreement from the party receiving the data. Moreover, a contractor may not have confidence that all Government employees will adequately protect confidential or proprietary information from disclosure.

Government Viewpoint

The Government does not want to get into the middle of a dispute between the data owner and the party that violates protections of that data. This provision is intended to provide the contractor—as the most interested party—with a more direct remedy against the party that engaged in the unauthorized conduct.

Solution

First, the contracting officer should consider a key fundamental concept—take possession of only that data which is absolutely necessary. This may alleviate the requirement for non-disclosure agreements entirely. Perhaps just the ability to review the data at the contractor's site is necessary.

If data is required, the Government could request that the data owner provide the data to the third party and obtain the appropriate non-disclosure agreements at that time. Some Government officials may not support this approach because of the potential that additional terms and conditions imposed by the IP owner on the third party will result in an unnecessary associated time delay or expense that will impact the performance of Government contracts.

Alternatively, the Government could notify the data owner before the data is being released and provide copies of the nondisclosure agreements to the data owner. The contractor should then seek the execution of nondisclosure agreements directly with the third-party recipient(s) of the data from the Government prior to the data's release. This way the data owner has a direct cause of action with the recipient(s).

Finally, another potential remedy to concerns about the treatment of contractor IP would be to establish management control systems to protect this information, similar to those used in formal source selections for the protection of proprietary proposal information. While this might be administratively burdensome to the Government, it may give the contractor increased faith that its proprietary data will be properly handled.

Issue 3-C: Specifically Negotiated License Rights[6]

Clauses

The 7013 and 7014 clauses permit the contracting officer to negotiate lesser rights than unlimited rights or GPR, as the parties consider appropriate, but no less than limited/restricted rights.

Industry Concern

Industry believes that contracting officers are acquiring unlimited rights in technical data when they are not needed and are refusing to negotiate when the Government's actual needs are for less than unlimited rights. This may be happening

---

[6] Also referred to as "special license rights."

because of the historical need for technical data to provide the ability to conduct competitive reprocurements of items or spare parts. Furthermore, even though the Government may have financial involvement, industry may have invested in the technology for decades and may refuse to provide any rights to technical data that include trade secrets. Another problem exists with the lack of specificity of legends under special license rights, where the contract is referenced but the specific license agreement is not identified. Later, it may be administratively difficult to protect the company's interests, when the players have changed and the contract is not readily available.

Government Viewpoint

It is DoD's policy to obtain only the minimum rights necessary. The standard provisions are a good starting place for negotiations, and it is incumbent on the contractor to inform the Government when it would like to deviate from the standard provisions. In order to begin such negotiations, it is necessary for the contractor to explicitly state what data it will deliver under the contract, and what rights it will deliver with the data.

Solution

As a preliminary matter, the parties should first confirm that the technical data or computer software at issue is related to noncommercial items or services. If the items or services are commercial, then the rights in the associated technical data are covered by the DFARS 252.227-7015 clause, and DoD policy is to accept the license customarily offered to the public for commercial computer software.

The Government and contractors should be encouraged to discuss data deliverables and rights early in the procurement cycle. Prior to 1995, less flexibility existed in the data rights clauses, and therefore, the Government often obtained the same rights in data no matter what the data was or what was actually needed by the Government. Today, however, contracting officers are free to negotiate special license rights for any developed data to make sure that the Government only acquires rights in the data that it needs.

Contracting officers can negotiate a contract clause under the specifically negotiated license rights arena that addresses the real needs of the Government. Such a clause might address

- escrowing, with third parties, critical technical data, computer source code, designs, and so on, whereby Government access would be limited to actual contingency or emergency circumstances;

- establishing a deferred right to acquire technical data under specific special circumstances;

- requiring advance notice of a change in the firm's or product's circumstances that might cause acquisition or logistic support problems;

◆ establishing the right to a "lifetime" (or until the next technology insertion occurs) buy if a product or technology is to be discontinued or the company is going out of business;

◆ limiting the use of the data to a particular component of any agency and/or to a particular program (e.g., DoD-purpose rights, service-purpose rights, agency-purpose rights, or program-purpose rights), and/or to a particular term of years;

◆ limiting the scope of the license to performing specified tasks or to making disclosures to specified kinds of recipients;

◆ agreeing to a separate services contract to provide technical assistance from the developer's engineers, if needed; and

◆ extending the time limit when GPR convert to unlimited rights.

Note that, in all cases, the Government is not permitted to accept less than limited rights in technical data nor less than restricted rights in computer software (however, less than restricted rights in computer software may be accepted if a waiver is obtained).

As discussed earlier, contracting officers should be firm in requiring a list in all proposals that clearly identifies the data that is proposed to be delivered and the associated rights offered to the Government for that data. With a clear list, the contracting officer and the offeror will have a full understanding of the areas in which IP or data discussions must take place. Because the terms of 7013 and 7014 allow flexibility during and after contract performance, contracting officers should be open to modifying the license terms when necessary.

Issue 3-D: Marking Requirements

Clauses

Under paragraph (f)(4), Special License Rights Markings, the 7013 and 7014 clauses provide a legend to be used for specifically negotiated licenses.

Industry Concern

The essential terms of the license are not included within the mandatory Special License Rights legend format. In addition, locating the official license in contract files that are years old, as well as personnel turnover, can make it difficult to be sure that the actual license will be adhered to.

Government Viewpoint

The Government wants to be fair in handling and protecting industry IP by adhering to appropriate legends on data. It is important that the universe of potential legends are restricted to a manageable number, so that DoD can effectively train its personnel regarding the restrictions associated with the well-established legends. In addition the Special License Rights legend provides for the insertion of appropriate license-identifying information. Furthermore, efforts are underway to ensure that all contract-related documents are readily available (e.g., on DoD-hosted Internet sites).

Solution

The contracting officer should, if feasible, include within the Special License Rights legend itself, in the space provided for the license identifier, the actual terms of the agreement[7] as in the following example:

> **Special License Rights**
>
> **The Government's rights to use, modify, reproduce, release, perform, display, or disclose these data are restricted by Contract No. _XXX_, License No. _YYY_ (This data is delivered with GPR limited to the Mark VI ammunition program). Any reproduction of technical data or portions thereof marked with this legend must also reproduce the markings.**

In doing so, the contractor must ensure that the descriptive language accurately represents the restrictions on the Government's uses. In all cases, the specifically negotiated license agreement must be incorporated into the contract in full text (e.g., by attachment), and the terms of that license (vice any paraphrasing used in the restrictive marking) will determine the Government's legal rights to use the delivered data. Furthermore, electronic contracting and digital storage will enable easier access and retrieval of the license.

Issue 3-E: Removal of Unjustified or Nonconforming Markings

Clauses

The 7013 and 7014 clauses—in paragraph (h), Removal of Unjustified and Nonconforming Markings—establish procedures and rights with respect to the removal of nonconforming markings and unjustified markings. A "nonconforming marking" is one that does not comply with the form or content requirements specified in the 7013 and/or 7014 clauses (e.g., the generic legend "proprietary"). An "unjustified marking" is one that does not accurately depict the Government's rights in the marked data (e.g., using a limited rights legend on GPR data).

---

[7] Copies of license agreements also must be incorporated into the contract and included in official contract files.

In some acquisitions, an IP issue may present itself for the first time when the Government is reviewing a deliverable for acceptance and discovers a restrictive legend that appears to be defective or inappropriate in some manner.

A "nonconforming" legend is one that does not comply with the form or substance required by the applicable DFARS marking requirements. The contracting officer should notify the contractor of any such nonconformities, which the contractor must then correct at its own expense. If the contractor fails to correct the marking within 60 days of receiving notice of the nonconformity, the Government may correct the marking at the contractor's expense.

An "unjustified" marking is one that does not accurately characterize the restrictions that apply to a particular deliverable. For example, if a restricted rights legend is placed on software for which the Government is entitled to receive GPR, that legend is unjustified (even if it conforms to the format and content for restricted rights legends). The procedures for reviewing and challenging unjustified legends are provided in DFARS 252.227-7019 for noncommercial computer software, and DFARS 252.227-7037.[8] During the challenge process, the Government must treat the disputed data as if it were subject to the rights category asserted by the contractor.

Industry Concern

Some in industry have reported that Government officials have inappropriately removed proprietary markings and legends.

Government Viewpoint

The Government needs the right to remove and/or correct nonconforming markings so that the delivery of data complies with the contract terms. Part of this responsibility involves correctly following the clause, which provides detailed procedures designed to ensure that the contractor's proprietary interests are balanced with the Government's need to engage in authorized uses of the data.

Solution

The acquisition team should be mindful of any action that could jeopardize the IP rights of the developer. They should not remove legends without following the procedures of the clause, so as not to incur legal and/or criminal liability. In keeping with the core IP principles (detailed in Chapter 1), the contracting parties should identify all data to be delivered and their respective data rights in the initial contract, thereby eliminating post-contract-award disputes.

---

[8] Based on 10 U.S.C. 2321. Note, for technical data pertaining to commercial items, there is a mandatory presumption that the commercial item was developed exclusively at private expense; see DFARS 227.7102 and 252.227-7037(b), which implements 10 U.S.C. §§ 2320(b)(1) and 2321(f).

Issue 3-F: Data with Omitted Markings

Clauses

The 7013 and 7014 clauses—in paragraph (f)—include the clear requirement for industry to include appropriate legends on data that qualify for such marking. In addition, the DFARS provides guidance for a contracting officer to approve a contractor's request for the reinstatement of inadvertently omitted markings. The request must be made within six months of delivery.

Industry Concern

Some in industry express concern that the six months may be too short a period for requesting the reinstatement of legitimate markings, particularly since the penalty for the delay is automatic conversion to unlimited rights.

Government Viewpoint

Since the importance of marking data is so critical to a company's economic value, great care should be taken to ensure their data is properly marked. Similarly, business-to-business proprietary marking is indeed required for the enforcement of rights and remedies in the commercial sector. It is fundamental to trade-secret law that the trade-secret owner should take reasonable steps to protect the trade secret. Doing business with the Government should be no different.

Solution

Since the marking of Government data is unique in form and substance to that typically used in the commercial world, it is possible that markings may be incorrect or missing. Contracting officers are free to extend this six-month period, but they are advised to do so under appropriate circumstances.

The contractor is required to identify, prior to award, all asserted restrictions on data it intends to deliver to the Government and to keep that list updated after award. Before making any delivery of technical data or computer software, the contractor should review these lists to ensure that markings on the data are consistent with the assertions in the list. Likewise, upon receipt of the deliverable, the Government should also compare lists with the markings on the data. Any discrepancies should be raised immediately.

Issue 3-G: Copyrights

Clauses

The third-party copyrighted data provision of the 7013 and 7014 clauses— in paragraph (d)—provides that data delivered under the contract must include appropriate licenses for copyrighted material.

Industry Concern

Contracting officers sometimes require unlimited rights to copyrighted material for data developed exclusively at Government expense. This gives the Government the right to disclose the data to anyone, including the contractor's competitors.

Government Viewpoint

Historically, when the Government pays for the entire development cost, it asserts unlimited rights in everything—even copyrighted material.

Solution

Only in the rarest of cases should the Government demand—over the IP owner's objection—more than GPR to copyrighted material, even if the material was developed entirely at Government expense.

There is a difference between providing a description of what has been done, and documenting the analyses and creative intuitive thought processes arriving at new theories/hypotheses. In copyrights, the Government owns the deliverable but not the creative work (similarly, buying a book at a bookstore does not grant the book owner the copyright in the book). The contracting officer should use the specifically negotiated license rights to reduce the rights in copyrighted material to take GPR only.

Issue 3-H: Government Purpose Rights

Clauses

The 7013 and 7014 clauses provide that, after a five-year period (unless otherwise negotiated), GPR "convert" to unlimited rights.

Industry Concern

The Government should allow industry to recoup its investment through the commercialization of data beyond a five-year period.

Government Viewpoint

Historically, the Government has wanted to limit the Government-purpose license period to support its life-cycle needs.

Solution

The contracting officer needs to be flexible by considering industry's investment in mixed-funding data. A contracting officer can allow a contractor to recoup its investment simply by allowing a time period longer than five years for the conversion of GPR to unlimited rights. This may be done at the time the contract is entered or during contract performance. The appropriate time period should be what is necessary to provide incentive for the contractor to commercialize the items, components, or processes. For negotiations of different types of license rights, contracting officers should consider using the contractor's customary commercial license, provided it grants the Government at least limited/restricted rights.

ISSUE CATEGORY 4: TECHNICAL DATA— COMMERCIAL ITEMS (DFARS 252.227-7015)

Issue 4-A: Emergency Repair and Overhaul

Clause

Under the Technical Data clause for commercial items,[9] the Government may release, disclose, or authorize the use of technical data for the emergency repair or overhaul of commercial items. In this context, the clause does not treat commercial software.

Industry Concern

Companies are concerned that their trade secrets embedded in technical data may be released to competitors under the rubric of an emergency. They are also concerned that the term "emergency" is ill-defined, such that almost any situation could be justified as an emergency, as it is dependent on the judgment of the involved Government official. Note that this issue is also associated with DFARS 252.227-7013 and the DFARS 252.227-7014 clauses.

Government Viewpoint

The Government needs to move immediately to make repairs in critical situations where, for example, an aircraft, submarine, or ship becomes immobile. In addition, these emergency procedures include a number of requirements that are designed to ensure that this use will not jeopardize the contractor's proprietary

---

[9] DFARS 252.227-7015(b)2(ii), Technical Data—Commercial Items.

interests (e.g., the recipient of the data must immediately destroy its copies of the data, and the contractor-owner must be notified).

Solution

The Government could request that the contractor propose an alternative for accommodating emergency repair and overhaul so that disclosure of data to third parties need not be required. If the contractor has a worldwide network of support (which many do), it may be that the contractor can provide the support needed in the time of an emergency, without disclosing data to another entity. It also can be helpful to negotiate a definition of the kind of situations that fall under the category of "emergency," thereby narrowing the scope of the exception.

Issue 4-B: Subcontractor Flow-Down

Clause

Prime contracts that include the DFARS 252.227-7013 clause for the purposes of the prime's noncommercial development of noncommercial technical data often do not include the DFARS 252.227-7015 clause, which covers technical data on commercial items.

Industry Concern

Because the prime contract does not include the DFARS 252.227-7015 clause, contractors believe they do not have the authority to flow the clause down to the subcontract.

Government Viewpoint

Typically, prime contracts are negotiated considering only the development of the major item and may not include this clause.

Solution

Because of the new emphasis on trying to insert commercial technology at all contracting echelons, it is now necessary for contracting officers to include both clauses (DFARS 252.227-7013 and DFARS 252.227-7015) in prime contracts for development, even if the prime contract item does not appear, on the surface, to be a commercial item. Further, prime contractors should ensure that DFARS 252.227-7015, which is not a required flow-down clause, is appropriately utilized in their subcontracts.

ISSUE CATEGORY 5: ROYALTY INFORMATION (FAR 52.227-6)

Issue 5-A: Copies of Current Licenses

Clause

Under the solicitation provisions for royalty information, [10] the contracting officer may request copies of license agreements that the contractor has signed with other firms.

Industry Concern

License agreements contain confidential terms and conditions and other business information that a firm would prefer not to disclose. Sometimes the mere existence of the license agreement is confidential.

Government Viewpoint

The Government is interested in knowing whether another agency has licensed the technology so that the Government does not pay a royalty for a patent to which it already has a royalty-free license. Also, for pricing analysis purposes, the Government may be interested in knowing the royalty rate.

Solution

The use of this clause is at the discretion of the contracting officer; hence, if it poses a significant problem, it can be removed. Alternatively, a contractor can redact the sensitive information in the license agreement before submitting a copy of the license agreement to the contracting officer.

ISSUE CATEGORY 6: DISCLOSURE OF INFORMATION (DFARS 252.204-7000)

Issue 6-A: Information Disclosure Constraints

Clause

The contractor is precluded from releasing, to anyone outside the contractor's organization, any unclassified information (regardless of medium) pertaining to any part of the contract or any program related to the contract, without the prior approval of the contracting officer.

---

[10] FAR 52.227-6, Royalty Information.

Industry Concern

This clause effectively prohibits a contractor's commercialization of technology without the Government's consent. The contractor is unable to provide information to a licensee or a subcontractor, even for contract performance requirements. Companies may feel that this clause is too broad and unduly restricts their ability to publish scientific results.

Government Viewpoint

The Government does not want the contractor to make public releases about the substance of a Government contract prior to the Government making any appropriate announcements, if the information has been determined to be sensitive and inappropriate for release to the public.

Solution

This clause, if used at all, should be limited to information specifically contained in contract deliverables that were developed under the contract. In contracts in which the clause is used, a special provision should be added permitting the contractor to license its own technology to third parties, or provide it to subcontractors for the performance of the contract, without Government consent.

ISSUE CATEGORY 7: DEFERRED DELIVERY OF TECHNICAL DATA OR COMPUTER SOFTWARE (DFARS 252.227-7026), DEFERRED ORDERING OF TECHNICAL DATA OR COMPUTER SOFTWARE (DFARS 252.227-7027), AND ADDITIONAL DATA REQUIREMENTS (FAR 52.227-16)

Issue 7-A: Deferred Ordering and Deferred Delivery

Clauses

These clauses provide for the deferred delivery and/or ordering of data generated under a contract.

Industry Concern

The open-ended right to order data at will causes industry a great deal of concern. In addition, how the Government interprets what data is "generated" under the contract leaves some fearful that proprietary information will be swept into the action. These clauses also require companies to warehouse all contract-related data for several years after acceptance of the contract deliverables.

Government Viewpoint

The Government has historically desired the ability to obtain any and all data developed and paid for by the Government, for years after contract completion. This desire was to ensure that the Government had adequate data and rights to assist in reprocurements.

Solution

The Government should include these clauses with caution, since they could subject the contractor to providing data later that may reveal trade secrets. The Government need not include the Deferred Ordering Clause at all. Even if the Government believes there is a possibility it may need access to contract-related data, the Government does not necessarily need to be assured of the data delivery. Instead, it might need only to be assured of its access to review the data at the contractor's facility.

Alternatively, the Government and industry may negotiate, prior to contract award, a special provision that states the Deferred Ordering Clause does not apply to certain types of data and software. This alternative requires the parties to consider what data they might want to order at a later date.

Regarding the use of deferred delivery, the parties should agree up front as to which specific data may be required.